T0043331

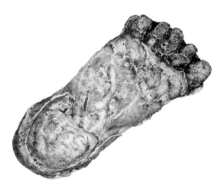

FIRST EDITION
Project Editor Mary Atkinson; **Art Editor** Karen Lieberman; **Senior Editor** Linda Esposito;
Deputy Managing Art Editor Jane Horne; **US Editor** Regina Kahney; **Production** Kate Oliver;
Picture Researchers Jo Carlill and Tom Worsley; **Illustrator** Pete Roberts;
Reading Consultant Linda Gambrell, PhD

THIS EDITION
Editorial Management by Oriel Square
Produced for DK by WonderLab Group LLC
Jennifer Emmett, Erica Green, Kate Hale, *Founders*

Editors Grace Hill Smith, Libby Romero, Michaela Weglinski;
Photography Editors Kelley Miller, Annette Kiesow, Nicole DiMella; **Managing Editor** Rachel Houghton;
Designers Project Design Company; **Researcher** Michelle Harris; **Copy Editor** Lori Merritt;
Indexer Connie Binder; **Proofreader** Larry Shea; **Reading Specialist** Dr. Jennifer Albro;
Curriculum Specialist Elaine Larson

Published in the United States by DK Publishing
1745 Broadway, 20th Floor, New York, NY 10019

A catalog record for this book
is available from the Library of Congress.
HC ISBN: 978-0-7440-6764-4
PB ISBN: 978-0-7440-6765-1

DK books are available at special discounts when purchased
in bulk for sales promotions, premiums, fundraising, or
educational use. For details, contact: DK Publishing Special Markets,
1745 Broadway, 20th Floor, New York, NY 10019
SpecialSales@dk.com

Printed and bound in China

The publisher would like to thank the following for their kind permission to reproduce their images:
a=above; c=center; b=below; l=left; r=right; t=top; b/g=background

Alamy Stock Photo: Kadumago 4-5, Adisha Pramod 32cla, Trinity Mirror / Mirrorpix 17tr, Xinhua 42cl;
CORBIS /Getty Images: Josef Scaylea 38b; **Dreamstime.com:** Alberto Agnoletto 14tl, Klomsky 16tl;
Getty Images / iStock: E+ / hadynyah 25clb, ilbusca 22, KenCanning 42tl, Mikael Males 43tr, Rolls Press/Popperfoto 17bl,
Royal Geographic Society 28tl, 29, timnewman 36tl; **Nature Picture Library:** Anup Shah 7br; **Shutterstock.com:** Berzina 25tr,
CloudVisual 12clb, Eseniy 17crb, Valerii Evlakhov 23tr, ilmarinfoto 18tl, K.E.V 23clb,
Philippe Clement 11tr, Savvapanf Photo 28cl, Igor Shoshin 33b, Sergey Uryadnikov 6tl, Yellow Cat 7tr; **TopFoto:** 16,
Crook / Fortean 1, 44, Fortean 13, 18-19, 31, 38t, 40-41, 42r, 43b, 45, PA Photos 30t, 39

Cover images: *Front & Spine:* **Shutterstock.com:** Daniel Eskridge; *Back:* **Getty Images:** DigitalVision Vectors / Big_Ryan clb,
DigitalVision Vectors / cpuga cla; **Shutterstock.com:** SofART cra

All other images © Dorling Kindersley

For the curious
www.dk.com

BEASTLY TALES

Malcolm Yorke

CONTENTS

Deadly Predator
Komodo dragons have a mouth full of sharp, serrated teeth. Their saliva contains a substance that keeps blood from clotting. So, once bleeding starts, it doesn't stop.

Natural Habitat
Komodo dragons are only found on a few Indonesian islands. Outsiders named them for Komodo Island, the island where they first saw them.

BELIEVE IT OR NOT!

All around the world, people tell stories about seeing mysterious monsters in remote places. Outsiders often accuse the storytellers of making things up. But sometimes people have experiences that prove to outsiders that the stories are true.

Few outsiders believed the stories about a man-like ape in Africa, a dragon in Indonesia, or a huge sea monster with long tentacles. However, everyone now recognizes these creatures as the mountain gorilla, the Komodo dragon, and the giant squid.

The Komodo dragon is a meat-eating lizard that can grow bigger than a person, but the outside world didn't know about it until 1910.

The Kraken of old Norwegian tales is now believed to be the giant squid, which can grow twice as long as a bus.

Just because something sounds strange doesn't mean it cannot be true. Could there be other large creatures still undiscovered in the world?

Giant of the Deep
It is extremely rare to see a giant squid. They live in deep ocean waters. Most of what we know about them comes from studying dead carcasses that washed up on beaches or floated to the ocean's surface.

Mountain Gorillas
These African animals were first discovered by European explorers in 1902.

Dark Waters
Six rivers flow into Loch Ness. They carry particles of peat from the surrounding soils. This makes the loch's water dark and murky—an excellent place for a strange creature to hide!

THE LOCH NESS MONSTER

"Dad! Dad! What's that in the loch?" shouted Jim Ayton. It was a calm summer's evening in 1963. Jim was working on his father's farm near Loch Ness, a lake in Scotland. He looked up to see a strange creature moving silently down the lake. It was huge! Jim had never seen anything like it before.

Loch Ness lies in northern Scotland.

Two people nearby heard Jim's shouts and rushed to join him and his father. The excited group wanted a closer look. They ran to the lake, climbed into a boat, and headed straight toward the creature.

Loch Ness
"Loch" is the Scottish Gaelic word for lake. Loch Ness is a long, narrow lake surrounded by mountains. It is in a part of Scotland where few people live.

The creature's head looked a bit like a horse's head, only bigger. Its neck stretched nearly 6 feet (2 m), as tall as a full-grown man. Its snake-like body was as long as a bus. Could it be the legendary Loch Ness monster that people had talked about for years?

Suddenly, the creature rose out of the water. Then, it dived. An enormous wave hit the small boat. It rocked and swirled around. Had the creature seen them? Was it about to attack?

Ancient Carving
Picts, ancient Scottish Highlanders, carved accurate pictures of animals in rocks. One image shows a huge water creature with a long neck and flippers.

A Deep Lake
If you were to view the lake, it would be hard to imagine that it has a depth of more than 700 feet (213 m)—that's deep enough to hide a 45-story building.

Lots of Water
Loch Ness holds more water than all of the lakes and rivers in England and Wales combined.

A few seconds later, the creature's head reappeared. It was farther away now. The monster seemed more frightened than ferocious! Then, it was gone. The men searched and searched for it, but they never saw it again.

It was 20 years before anyone heard the story about what had happened that day. Jim and his father didn't think many people would believe them. But the Aytons and their friends are not the only people who claim to have seen this mysterious monster.

This photograph, taken by monster hunter Anthony Shiels 14 years after the Aytons' sighting, seems to show the monster just as the Aytons described it.

Saint Columba is featured on this stained-glass window in a Scottish castle chapel.

One of the earliest known sightings was made more than 1,400 years ago by Saint Columba, a traveling Irish holy man. Legends tell how, in 565 CE, the saint saw a "water monster" attack a swimmer in Loch Ness. When the saint ordered it to leave the swimmer alone, the monster retreated immediately.

Loch Legends
There are many legends of water monsters living in other Scottish lakes. The Scottish people call these monsters kelpies.

The Loch Ness monster first became famous in 1933, after a road was built around the steep sides of the Loch Ness valley. Tourists could now explore this remote area for the first time. It was not long before reports of monster sightings began appearing in newspapers all around the world.

Drive-By
The 1933 sighting was by a couple driving past the lake. They claimed to have seen something that looked like a dragon or prehistoric monster. Their story later appeared in a newspaper.

The monster is the star attraction on this 1930s postcard from Loch Ness.

Fantastic Footprints

In December 1933, the *Daily Mail* newspaper hired Marmaduke Wetherell to find the Loch Ness monster. After a few days, the actor/director/ big game hunter found giant footprints. The prints were later discovered to have been made with a stuffed hippopotamus foot.

Spotting the monster soon brought rewards. Newspapers would pay a lot of money for a photograph of the monster—even if it was blurred! Fortune seekers, scientists, and monster enthusiasts swarmed around the loch, all wanting to take the best monster picture ever.

LOCH NESS INV

342 CBT

Over the years, the searchers used more and more modern equipment. In 1972, an underwater camera produced a close-up of a strange object in the loch. When scientists used a special computer to sharpen up the image, they thought they saw a flipper. "Monster fever" hit a new height.

24/7
In the 1960s, a group of people started the Loch Ness Investigation Bureau. They watched the loch for 10 years.

Credible Claims
People claiming to have seen the Loch Ness monster include lawyers, priests, police officers, and even a Nobel Prize winner.

More than 100 scientists met to discuss this 1975 photo, which supposedly shows a Loch Ness flipper.

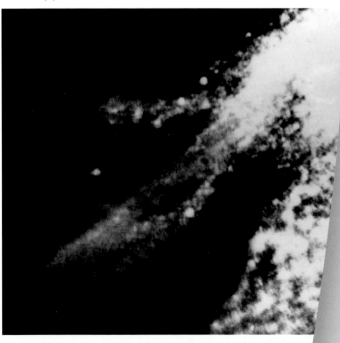

Nickname
The Loch Ness monster is nicknamed Nessie.

Sonar Scanners
A sonar scanner sends out sound waves. The sound waves bounce back off objects in their way, making a picture of the objects on the sonar screen.

The underwater photograph seems to show a flipper, but no one can be sure because the image is so grainy. It is hard to see or to take a photograph in the lake water because it is full of tiny pieces of peat, or dead plant material.

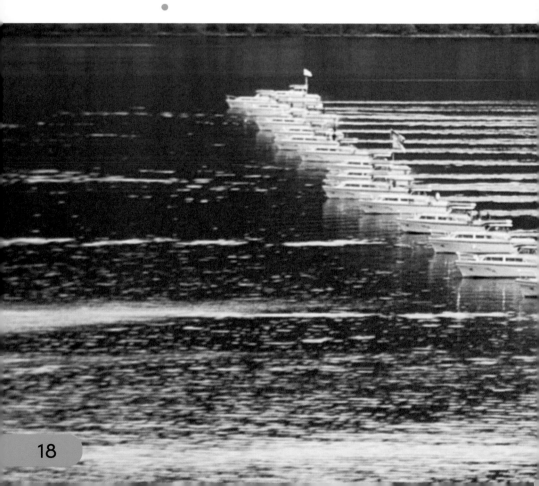

In 1987, a team of scientists searched the loch with high-tech equipment for a project called Operation Deepscan. A line of 19 boats, each fitted with a sonar scanner, moved up the loch. What they discovered amazed them.

Evidence?
The three mysterious objects discovered on sonar in the 1987 Operation Deepscan search could not be identified. And when people went back to study them further, they couldn't find them.

Some scans showed huge objects moving deep in the lake. The objects were bigger than sharks but smaller than whales. Were they huge fish? Or was it a family of Loch Ness monsters? Again, the murky water kept the scientists from knowing the answer.

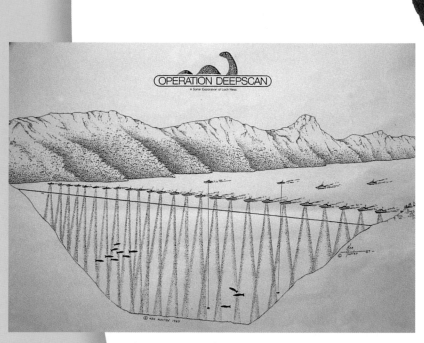

This diagram shows how the boats with sonar scanners moved in a line so that no part of the loch would be missed.

Without clear pictures, scientists must rely on people's descriptions to know what the monster looks like. It seems that the creature has a long, thin neck; a bulky body with four flippers; and a long, powerful tail.

No animal living today fits this description. However, one prehistoric creature does.

ANOTHER SEARCH
In 2003, researchers searched the lake for the Loch Ness. They used satellites and 600 sonar beams. They did not find any evidence of a large animal in the lake.

Artists used eyewitness descriptions to design this model of the Loch Ness monster.

This fossil skeleton of *Cryptocleidus* is twice as long as an adult person.

Cryptocleidus
The first *Cryptocleidus* fossil was discovered in 1892. It was not a dinosaur, but it lived alongside them.

Cryptocleidus was a plesiosaur: a huge fish-eating reptile that lived in the sea. Some people think it looked a lot like the Loch Ness monster. However, *Cryptocleidus* is thought to have disappeared from Earth 70 million years ago! Could it have lived on unnoticed?

Is the Loch Ness monster a survivor from the dinosaur age? Or were the people who saw it simply fooled by boats, logs, shadows, or giant eels? Could some of the sightings be the result of practical jokes? No one knows the truth—yet.

DNA Dive

In 2019, a team of scientists from Otago University in New Zealand announced the results of their DNA study of the Loch Ness waters. They found evidence of about 3,000 species—but no plesiosaurs and no monsters. The scientists theorize that the Loch Ness monster might actually be a giant eel.

From a distance, it would be easy to mistake this log for a monster. Could everyday things like this explain some of the Loch Ness monster sightings?

The Highest in the World
At 29,028 feet (8,848 m), Mount Everest is the world's highest mountain. It takes weeks to climb to the top.

Believers
According to Sherpa tradition, the yeti will only show itself to people who believe in it.

YETI

Even the police felt afraid when they saw the footprints of the beast that attacked Lhakpa Dolma.

In 1974, teenager Lhakpa lived in a Nepalese village high in the Himalayan mountains. Each day, she climbed partway up Mount Everest to graze a herd of yaks, a type of cattle.

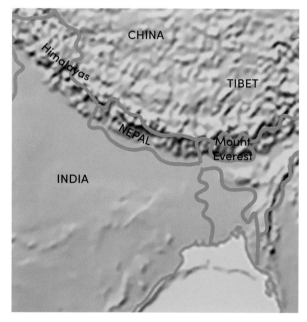

Himalayan mountains

Lhakpa saw few people on the steep mountain paths. Only Buddhist monks and nuns who chose to build their monasteries far from towns and cities lived this high up.

Lhakpa had heard tales of the yeti, an ape-like beast said to live in the Himalayas. But the mountains stretched for thousands of miles. She never expected to see one herself.

Many Nepalese people live on the slopes of the Himalayas.

Valuable Creatures
People living among the Himalayas rely on yaks for many things. These hardy beasts provide meat, dairy products, clothing, and fuel.

Like these people, Lhakpa's family were Sherpas—people who first came from eastern Tibet to Nepal around 400 years ago.

One day, as Lhakpa grazed the herd, she noticed that the yaks seemed restless. She led them to a clear, snow-fed stream.

Suddenly, Lhakpa heard a strange, deep grunt. She whirled around as a huge, two-legged creature came rushing toward her. It was a yeti! Terrified, she broke into a run.

But the yeti grabbed Lhakpa in its long, hairy arms. She screamed and kicked, but the yeti was too strong. Then the beast dropped her into the icy stream and turned on her yaks.

With powerful blows, it quickly
killed three of the enormous beasts.
Lhakpa crawled out of the stream
and ran home as fast as she could.
When the police investigated the
scene, they found the yeti's large
footprints—but not the yeti.

Eric Shipton
Mountaineer Eric Shipton was on an expedition to climb Mount Everest when he took the first ever photograph of a yeti footprint.

Ages Old
The search for the yeti dates back to 326 BCE. Alexander the Great, an ancient Macedonian king, had heard stories of the mysterious creature and wanted to find him.

Lhakta's story is similar to many other tales of the yeti reported by people living in the Himalayas. Mountaineers, drawn by the challenge of exploring the world's highest mountain range, have also told chilling tales of this ape-like beast. In 1951, mountaineer Eric Shipton and his party were exploring an unknown part of the Himalayas when they came across a line of strange footprints in the snow.

Michael Ward, one of Eric Shipton's climbing companions, compares his own footprints, on the right, with those of the creature.

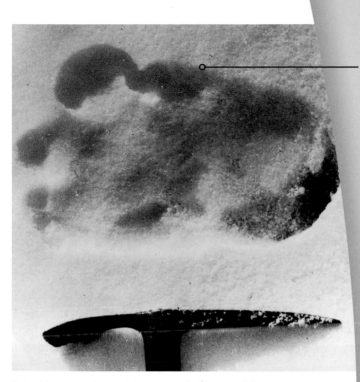

Eric Shipton placed his 13-inch (33-cm) ice ax in this photograph to show the size of the footprint.

Pricey Pictures
In 2014, Eric Shipton's photos of yeti footprints sold at auction for over $8,000.

The footprints looked similar to human footprints—but they were twice as wide. They had sunk much deeper into the snow than the climbers' boot prints, so they must have been made by an incredibly heavy creature. Most amazing of all, the clear toe prints showed that the creature was walking barefoot in the freezing snow!

Expensive Search
In 1953, the *Daily Mail* newspaper sent an expedition to Nepal to find the yeti. It cost more than a million dollars in today's money. The searchers found no proof that the yeti existed.

Don Whillans
Hoping to get more than a glimpse, Whillans repeatedly peeked out from his tent at night. The creature returned! He saw it bound along on all fours and head for a cliff.

A Beast Called Yeti
The name "yeti" comes from the Sherpa words "yeh teh," which mean "that thing." The abominable snowman is another name for the yeti.

In 1970, another mountaineer had an even closer encounter with a yeti. Don Whillans was climbing in the Himalayas when a Sherpa guide called out, "Yeti coming!"

The yeti seems skilled at surviving on its own in a frozen environment (photograph shows model).

Don looked up, but only caught a quick look at the ape-like figure before it disappeared behind a ridge.

The next day, Don found the creature's footprints in the snow. They were about the same size as his boot prints. The Sherpa guide told him that the prints were made by a baby yeti.

A drawing of a yeti based on eyewitness descriptions

Namesake
The yeti crab, which lives deep in the ocean, is named for the famous monster. White hairlike structures cover its arms.

A yeti illustration from a French magazine

Later that night, Don saw the creature again. He was looking out of his tent into bright moonlight when it came loping along. It headed for a clump of trees and began pulling the branches.

Don grabbed his binoculars, but the creature suddenly noticed him and ran across the mountain and out of sight.

The number of yeti sightings caught the interest of some scientists. They studied photos and plaster casts of yeti footprints, then compared them with other animal footprints. They decided that the yeti prints could not have been made by a bear, an ape, an antelope, or any other known animal.

Monster Mania
Fascination with the yeti has inspired many stories. Some are serious news articles, while others are just good fun.

Could It Be?

In 2010, hunters in China caught an unusual animal they claimed was the yeti. The creature turned out to be a civet, a small cat-like animal that had lost its hair from disease.

A Scientific Search

In 2017, scientists tested bone, hair, skin, and teeth samples that were believed to be from the yeti. Tests showed that the samples belonged to different types of bears and a dog.

Aside from footprints, little evidence of the yeti has been found. There was excitement when a Nepalese monk gave a yeti scalp to Sir Edmund Hillary, one of the first men to climb Mount Everest.

Hillary handed the scalp over to scientists. It turned out to be a fake made of goat-antelope hair.

But yeti footprints are still being found. In 1992, Julian Freeman-Atwood found footprints on a glacier that no one had climbed for 30 years.

Will the mystery of the yeti ever be solved? What sort of creature is it? Where does it sleep? How does it find enough food on the snow-covered mountains? Maybe you will be the one who discovers the answers!

The yeti scalp given to Sir Edmund Hillary

Yeti footprints have been discovered on other mountains in Asia, as well as the Himalayas. These footprints found by Julian Freeman-Atwood were on a glacier in Mongolia.

BIGFOOT

Albert Ostman was expecting a quiet time when he headed into a forest near Vancouver, Canada, for a camping trip in 1924.

But one night, Albert claimed, he woke with a jolt. Someone or something was lifting him up inside his sleeping bag! For hours, he was bumped and bounced around as something carried him over rough ground.

Room to Hide
Forests cover around 340,000 square miles (881,000 sq km) of the Pacific Northwest.

When daylight came, Albert got a look at his captor—and it wasn't alone!

Four huge, hairy beasts—three adults and a child—surrounded him. They looked half ape and half human. To Albert's relief, they did not hurt him, but for six days he was their prisoner.

Then, one day, one of the beasts became ill. As he rolled on the ground in pain, Albert made his escape.

The mysterious bigfoot is said to live in forests in the Pacific Northwest.

Albert Ostman photographed 33 years after his capture

Back in Vancouver, locals told Albert that his captors were bigfeet. These mysterious creatures have been sighted thousands of times in the forests of the Pacific Northwest.

A bigfoot is said to look similar to a yeti, although it could be even bigger. Some people have reported seeing bigfeet that were 8 feet (2.4 m) tall. The creatures are covered in hair and have flat faces, short necks, and wide shoulders.

Bigfoot's Many Names
Native Americans have told stories of bigfeet for centuries. Different tribes give the creature different names, such as Sasquatch or Oh-mah-ah.

A bigfoot has never been caught, dead or alive, but in 1967, two California men claimed that they captured one on film.

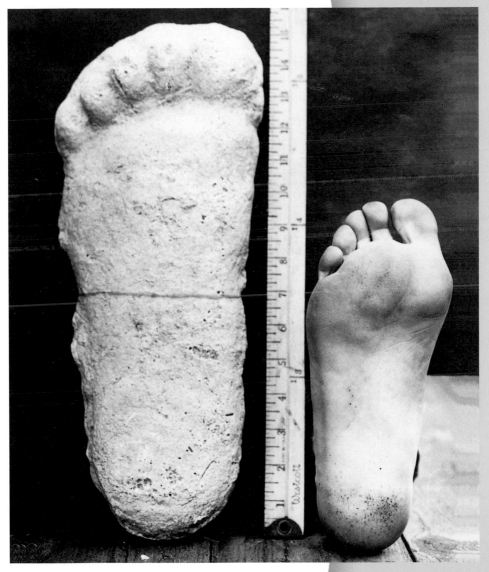

Comparing a possible bigfoot footprint (left) with an adult man's foot (right) shows how the creature got its name.

According to Roger Patterson, he and a friend set off on horseback on October 20, 1967, to find a bigfoot. Armed with a movie camera, they went searching in an area where there had already been some sightings.

They were riding alongside a stream when they rounded a corner and saw a bigfoot by the water's edge. Roger's horse reared up, throwing Roger to the ground. He jumped up and began filming.

The bigfoot ran toward the forest. Roger ran after it, filming the whole time. Some scientists thought the film was a fake, but they couldn't prove it.

These four photographs are from the actual film shot by Roger Patterson.

A Real Giant
A giant bigfoot did once exist, but it lived far from the Pacific Northwest. Based on fossil evidence, *Gigantopithecus blacki* lived in Southeast Asia. It was about 10 feet (3 m) tall and weighed almost 600 pounds (272 kg). It went extinct hundreds of thousands of years ago.

Experts in the United States and Russia studied the way the bigfoot moved. They decided that it would be very difficult for anyone in a fur suit to run in such a natural way.

Roger had made plaster casts of the bigfoot's footprints. The casts showed that the creature's feet were 14.5 inches (37 cm) long. Each foot had five toes, like a human foot, but the sole of the foot was much flatter.

Roger Patterson holding the plaster casts of the bigfoot's footprints

The same year, logger Glen Thomas claims he saw three bigfeet farther north in Oregon, USA. The largest one was moving a pile of huge rocks. Finally, it reached a nest of marmots. From behind the trees, Glen watched the bigfoot eat the animals one by one.

Later, investigators found that the rocks had been moved recently and that marmots did nest in that area.

marmot

Bigfoot Food
Judging from supposed eyewitness stories, it seems that bigfeet eat mainly plants, but they have also been spotted eating fish and small animals, such as marmots.

Glen Thomas on the rocks where he saw the bigfeet

Since then, more and more people have produced evidence of bigfeet. In 1995, a forest patrol officer in Washington, USA, claimed that he heard splashes and turned around to see a bigfoot looking straight at him.

One of the photographs taken by a forest patrol officer in 1995

Luckily, he had a camera with him and was able to take clear photographs. Experts argue about whether or not the photographs are real.

No one has collected absolute proof that bigfeet exist, but people have collected quite a bit of evidence. Tape recordings show that bigfeet grunt, whistle, roar, bark, and howl. Thousands of footprints have been found in mud, sand, and snow.

What should we do next? Many people believe we should just leave them alone.

What do you think?

Bigfoot Fakes
Some people have dressed up in bigfoot suits as a joke or to sell pictures to newspapers. However, the fact that one story is false does not mean that they all are.

Eyewitness Accounts
In the past 50 years, there have been more than 10,000 reported sightings of a bigfoot in the continental United States.

GLOSSARY

Abominable snowman
Another name for the yeti (see yeti)

Bigfoot
A large, hairy, ape-like beast that some people believe lives in Pacific Northwestern forests

Cryptocleidus
[krip-toe-KLIE-duss]
A plesiosaur that lived in the sea around Scotland 70 million years ago (see plesiosaur)

Evidence
Anything used to prove that something is true

Eyewitness
A person who says they have seen (witnessed) a particular event

Glacier
A huge mass of ice that slides downhill very slowly, often carving out a valley as it moves

Himalayas
The world's highest mountain range. It runs through India, Nepal, Tibet, and other countries.

Kelpie
A water monster with a horse-shaped head that some people believe lives in Scottish rivers and lakes

Kraken
A sea monster in Norwegian myths, now believed to be a giant squid

Loch
A Scottish lake

Loch Ness monster
A large monster that some people believe lives in Loch Ness, Scotland

Mountaineer
A person who climbs mountains

Plaster cast
A model made by pouring plaster into a shape and letting it harden

Plesiosaur
A large swimming reptile with a long neck and four flippers that swam in the sea millions of years ago (see *Cryptocleidus*)

Prehistoric
Anything from before written human history

Sasquatch
A name for bigfoot that comes from a Native American (Salish) word, meaning hairy man (see bigfoot)

Sherpas
People originally from eastern Tibet now living in Nepal

Sonar scanner
A machine that sends out sound waves and analyzes their echoes to build up a picture of an object

Yak
A type of cattle with long, thick hair found in the Himalayas

Yeti
A hairy, ape-like beast that many people believe lives in the Himalayas and the mountains of Mongolia

INDEX

QUIZ

Answer the questions to see what you have learned. Check your answers in the key below.

1. The Kraken is said to be a huge sea monster. What is it really?

2. Who made the earliest known sighting of the Loch Ness monster?

3. What kind of prehistoric creature fits the description of the Loch Ness monster?

4. Where does the yeti supposedly live?

5. What is another name for the yeti?

6. What possible evidence of a yeti has been found?

7. Where have bigfeet been sighted?

8. What are two other names bigfeet have been called?

1. A giant squid 2. Saint Columba 3. A huge reptile (*Cryptocleidus*)
4. The Himalayas 5. The abominable snowman 6. Footprints
7. The Pacific Northwest 8. Sasquatch and Oh-mah-ah